SELF-EDITING

ON

A PENNY

A COMPREHENSIVE GUIDE

ASHLYN FORGE

Copyright © 2014 Ashlyn Forge

Published in Japan

Cover Images ©

Cover Design by KM Writing & Design

http://www.ashlynforge.com

The text of this book was set in Garamond.

First Edition March 2015

1

ISBN-13: 978-1508460664

CONTENTS

PREFACE

If you're thinking, "I'm barely literate. I'm not an avid reader. Grammar makes me sweat, so much so that I have been asked if I'm really a native English speaker. I don't know a comma splice from a hole in the wall. Can I still become a writer?"

Then the answer is yes—and no.

To put it bluntly, a good story presented with poor editing and typos is like a good meal served on toilet paper. It'll still taste good, but it'll be harder to sell; and those who do eat it do so with trepidation and a possible cringe.

Your story is art. It *deserves* more. You wouldn't serve your specialty on paper plates so don't give your reader a less-than-perfect book riddled with errors.

Good storytelling is paramount and although proper grammar does not a good author make…it sure helps.

The following chapters provide you not only with some cost-effective shortcuts, but also methods to help you clean up some messy areas and lighten your burdensome self-publishing load.

Before we begin, know that there is no *self* in self-publishing. Equally, there is no *self* in self-editing. Don't try to do it all alone—even superheroes have help.

Sooner or later you will need to show others your work and get feedback. You will also need the one thing no amount of money can buy: **sober expectations**.

Self-Editing on a Penny will teach you how to self-edit, self-edit well, and do it all either in budget or free.

This book hopes to touch base on important (yet easily overlooked) grammar points, misused words, and creative-writing techniques.

It is written from the perspective of an indie author who has used both *professional* editors and *cost-effective*—even *free*—methods to edit.

I've taken one for the team, so you don't have to…. You're welcome.

WHY SELF-EDIT?

Self-editing? Isn't editing what an editor is for?

There are many reasons to self-edit.

Here is the first warning. No, you cannot self-edit and then *publish* right away. When it's our own work, we don't have the ability to be critical and objective enough to edit perfectly.

That being said, we *can* self-edit and reduce professional editing costs. We *can* also self-edit and couple it with other methods in order to make the edit *free*.

Bottom line, your WIP (Work In Progress) is not officially a final draft until you self-edit. You will no doubt go through the manuscript multiple times. Pace yourself so that you don't burn out and grow tired of it.

Here is another very important factor with regards to editing: there are three major edits: a content edit, a line edit, a proofread. Skimp on one *at your own peril*.

Often times, the first edit (content edit) is overlooked—authors simply skip it. Line editors will *not* tell an author the story is bad. *That is not their job.* Their job is to make the sentences *coherent.* Equally, a proofreader will be even less likely to blow the whistle and say, "Hey, this garbage needs a lot more work."

Basically, you might be strutting around unaware your zipper is open, proud as ever of your manuscript—not realizing others are 'speechless' for the wrong reasons.

Someone incredibly compassionate and friendly might pull you aside and tell you the truth. Most won't. Art is subjective and many people don't want to go out of their way to make you uncomfortable. They will do the specific job you requested and call it a day.

So *please* self-edit; please go slowly; and please don't cut corners if you can afford it.

REASONS TO SELF-EDIT

- Lower the cost of editing: When you self-edit, you reduce an editor's burden and therefore the editor might charge you much less. If a piece is especially awful, an editor might even refuse. By polishing that manuscript beforehand, you not only put an editor at ease, but you might essentially be getting a cheaper edit. Also, because there are many types of edits, a good self-edit might mean you don't have to invest money in each and every one, thus reducing your cost. Supplemented with a professional editor or otherwise, a proper self-edit can save you a lot of time and money, and help you hone your craft.

- Improve your writing: Self-editing is a great way to hone your skills. You learn something new each time you edit. The path is not easy, but with each new technique you learn, you become a stronger writer.

- Protect yourself: There are more than enough fake (and bad) editors out there. The more you know about grammar and the editing process, the easier it is for you to spot phonies and save yourself a world of suffering. Take it from me, because even now, two years later, I'm still eating my hat.

- Write faster: Sometimes those of us who care about smooth writing and good prose *know* we aren't writing as well as we'd like. That leads to self-doubt. It also leads to getting stuck in areas where we should never have been in the first place—writing yourself into a corner, for example. A good grasp of grammar and the rules of creative-writing will make you far more confident while providing you with the knowledge to make that first draft shine. Oh, it'll still stink (all drafts are bad), but it'll certainly shine.

ASHLYN FORGE

1. GETTING STARTED

Chances are the bulk of your publishing cost will go into editing. Here are some guidelines that will serve you on your self-editing journey.

Rule #1: There is no such thing as a cheap editor.
Someone starting out who might not be as confident might edit for free or out of the goodness of his/her heart, but that doesn't mean you'll get something for nothing: you will be a guinea pig. You've just donated your body (of work) to science.

Cheap editing = poor editing. As editing is rather time-consuming and editors have bills to pay, if you get a cheaper edit, it's likely the editor is simply not very good. OR, if the editor is good, he/she might have a heavy workload. That means your manuscript is just one of many to zip through before the month is out. Editors deserve a decent wage, so if you hire an editor, expect to pay from the latter end of hundreds to actual thousands.

Rule #2: Never use just one source (editing source).
Other than the technical, edits are **opinions** and you'll need a few before it's all said and done.

Rule #3: Leave your family out of this. A family is a family, not a company, and certainly not a *publishing* company. Self-publishing is a sometimes stressful journey. Go home to your family to rest, not to publish more. Family members tend to build you up, sometimes when they shouldn't. It's not always objective.

Rule #4: *Do not* defend your work. If an editor tells you something, take it or leave it, ask a question if you have to, but don't defend your work to him/her. Being defensive means you aren't objective and therefore high maintenance. It doesn't matter what you *tried* to convey. You obviously didn't do it well. Getting other opinions also means you can see what parts of the editor's critique were subjective.

TYPES OF EDITS

There are three main types of edits you will encounter. They are often called by different names but there are basically three. If you do encounter a different name, be sure to ask what each aspect of the edit will entail.

- content edit

- line edit

- proofread

1. Getting Started

A **development edit** is the same as a **content edit**. It's just what it sounds like, an editing of the content of your story. You may run into a **manuscript assessment** here also. This is where someone reads your story and tells you what's wrong with it. There might be positive feedback here, but essentially the job is to help you hammer out character flaws, plot holes, pacing issues, and so on. You *do not* want to skimp on this area as this is the core of your story.

A **copyedit** usually includes a **line edit** and proofreading but a line edit is focusing on the nuts and bolts: grammar, syntax, and word usage. This is probably the hardest area for an author who is weak at grammar. It's not as frightening as it looks, however. Latter chapters will show you some tips on how to go about it effectively.

Lastly, the **proofread,** which sometimes gets put under **copyedit**. This is of course one of the most important areas with regards to a reader being able to enjoy your work. Remember that meal served on toilet paper? Well, consider typos the small strands of hair a reader will encounter as they read. One or two can be overlooked, but more...not so much. A random typo can take someone out of the story and ruin the experience. A proofreader is important but a proofreader is only human, and it's rare any one person can catch each and every single error. We'll go over how to tighten up that proofread as well.

ASHLYN FORGE

2. LINE EDITING

Usually a **line edit** comes *after* a **content edit**. If you do go with an editor, please make sure a line edit comes *second*. That is because a content edit might have you taking out entire chapters, so it is a waste to edit the grammar only to throw some bits away.

With self-editing, however, you need to do the line editing first. That is because you will have to show this to someone and it's sometimes very difficult to read a story that's held together on wishful thinking and optimism rather than actual punctuation and proper spelling.

You will have to seek out feedback, so show everyone you are serious about your work. It's okay to have some errors but before you show your manuscript to another set of human eyes, let's tidy it up a bit. In this area, we'll touch on the basics of *line edits* as well as some grammar points that are often overlooked or misused.

ASHLYN FORGE

2-1. GRAMMAR & PUNCTUATION

Grammar goes a long way. And **grammar** can get rather complex. For the sake of keeping with simplicity, we'll go into the much needed (and often neglected) basic grammar here.

This book won't have too many unfamiliar words in an effort to not scare you away. It is in your best interest, however, to become familiar with the official terms and understand them.

For more in-depth grammar, please consult a grammar book in conjunction with this comprehensive guide.

Grammar is quite frightening to some people, as being ridiculed for simple mistakes is sometimes a source of shame. Although this book will take you through it rather slowly, it is *imperative* you learn it better if you intend to publish independently.

So after dipping your toe into this book, please seek out more information on grammar and jump right in.

As far as grammar books go, I've found that style guides are rather dry and hard to navigate. Your ideal grammar book should be short; it should give you a lot of examples; and it should perhaps provide a test after each chapter.

Grammar isn't just about improving your writing. It's also about staying safe. The biggest problem with not having a good enough grasp on grammar is that even if you get a sample-edit from a would-be editor, if your own handle of grammar is weak, you will have no real idea if that edit was good or bad.

I used professional editors on both of my debut novels (*In Liam's Wake: The Makeshift Soldier I* and *From Johann to Tannenbaum*) which were released together. Even now when I go back and read them, I see a lot I would have edited differently and they saw separate editors and racked up quite a bit of money.

Save yourself; brush up on grammar.

Here are some basic grammar points to look out for.

DIALOGUE TAGS

A basic dialogue tag you'll see in any book is:

> He said, "

This format is typical. So here are some key things to remember: wherever there is dialogue in a paragraph, all the action in that paragraph *must* belong to the one with the dialogue.

This is *bad*—two people in one paragraph:

Large paragraph:

> Beverly made her way to the door. She didn't look back. John called out to her, "Where are you going?" He hurried after her. "Hey!" "I'm leaving. Isn't that obvious?" Beverly yelled as she marched across the lawn, brand new high heels be damned.

Small paragraph:

> Beverly made her way to the door. John called out to her, "Where are you going?"

We don't know who is talking. Does the dialogue belong to Beverly or John? Therefore, big or small, separate one person per paragraph.

This is *good*:

Large Paragraph:

> Beverly made her way to the door. She didn't look back.
>
> John called out to her, "Where are you going?" He hurried after her. "Hey!"
>
> "I'm leaving. Isn't that obvious?" Beverly yelled as she marched across the lawn, brand new high heels be damned.

Small Paragraph:

> Beverly made her way to the door.
>
> John called out to her, "Where are you going?"

This is the typical format of any novel: the first line is indented by about five spaces.

> Beverly made her way to the door. She didn't look back.
> John called out to her, "Where are you going?" He hurried after her. "Hey!"

This is bad:

> John grabbed Beverly by the arm and swung her around. She yanked herself free. "You can't leave without answering me!"

This is good:

> John grabbed Beverly by the arm and swung her around.
>
> She yanked herself free.
>
> "You can't leave without answering me!" John said.

Things to remember:

> Keep one paragraph per person.
>
> Clearly indicate who is talking.
>
> Indent the first line of each paragraph.

SAID IS DEAD

Some say 'said' is dead and an author should avoid using this dialogue tag. Others still cling to it, rejecting alternatives. Whether you choose to abolish 'said' from your work or mix it in with various other dialogue tags—whispered, called, etc.—it's a good tool to have.

It's important to keep one person per dialogue so you do not confuse the reader. In some cases, said (and other dialogue tags) can be removed entirely *if* the paragraph makes the speaker clear.

For example:

> John stood, hands on his hips. "You can't leave."

In this case, we know who is talking by who the action belongs to. Take care when using this method as you can fall into the trap of giving your characters too much motion. My recommendation is to use dialogue tags. When no emotions or other tags fit, please consider 'said.' It is very common and most readers barely notice it.

HOW TO FORMAT DIALOGUE

John said, "Capital letter first."

"Hi," John said, "how are you?"

"Hi," John said. "How are you?"

"Hi," said Kathy. "How are you?"

"Hi," said Kathy, "how are you?"

He said, "Capital letter first."

"Hi," he said, "how are you?"

"Hi," he said. "How are you?"

"Why are you telling me this?" she asked.

"Oh no!" she shouted. (But "Oh no!" She jumped to her feet. *Jump* is not a dialogue tag therefore *She* is capitalized.)

She asked, "Why not?"

John said, "For long passages that might be very tiring and cumbersome to the reader, you can split it up into multiple paragraphs. If you need more than two paragraphs, consider the dialogue might become exhausting for the reader. You split it up like this. Leave this paragraph without an end-quote.

"Open another quote on the first line of the new paragraph. Continue your dialogue here. Everything in here is John's dialogue. Then when you are finally finished, close the quotation mark like so."

Alternative dialogue tags include: whispered, called, shouted, mumbled, quipped, and snapped.

They do not include: laughed, griped, shrugged, or sighed.

There are many more, so please fiddle around with it.

COMMA

The 'comma' is by far one of the hardest to use. As daunting as it might appear, the comma is quite basic. Contrary to popular belief, no sentence can continue indefinitely thanks to the aid of a comma. Limiting your comma usage and familiarizing yourself with it can help strengthen your sentences.

Hopefully this knowledge will also help you avoid lengthy and cumbersome run-ons.

Use a comma between two or more coordinate adjectives if the adjectives can stand alone and they are interchangeable.

He looked at the bold, beautiful sky.

Adjectives: **bold, beautiful**. They can stand alone if separated. Their positioning can also be switched.

He looked at the beautiful sky. (acceptable)

He looked at the bold sky. (acceptable)

He looked at the beautiful, bold sky. (acceptable)

He looked up at the bold **and** beautiful sky.

Therefore, when combined it becomes:

He looked at the bold, beautiful sky. (correct)

Next compare two more sentences. One uses a comma and the other does not.

The raggedy, old hat rested on the chair.

Vs.

He ate the lightly toasted bread.

First consider:

The raggedy, old hat rested on the chair.

The raggedy hat rested on the chair. (acceptable)

The old hat rested on the chair. (acceptable)

The old, raggedy hat rested on the chair. (acceptable)

The following sentence does not use a comma, however.

He ate the lightly toasted bread.

He ate the lightly bread. (unacceptable)

He ate the toasted bread. (acceptable)

He ate the toasted lightly bread. (unacceptable)

The first sentence is unacceptable, while the second one is fine. Therefore, there's no need for a comma in this situation. The correct sentence is the original:

He ate the lightly toasted bread.

Use commas after time.

In 1996, he traveled the world.

In time, he relented and married.

Eventually, he gave up on trying to make it work.

Finally, she shoved him into the pit.

Use commas for afterthoughts.

Today he looked worried, though he tried to play it off.

He refused to get upset, not because of this jerk.

She still loved him, criminal record and all.

He managed to climb out, finally catching his breath.

Use the comma when listing *three* things or more, but not for two things.

She bought eggs and sugar.

He bought two hens, a bat, and a pizza.

Use a comma when talking to someone.

Nice to meet you, John.

Where are you going, jerk?

Get out of my way, Robert.

Mary, that's dangerous.

Use the comma for interruptions.

Ms. Bailey, tired and afraid, crouched down beside the boulder.

Use the comma for dates.

January 1, 2001

Monday, January 1, 2001

Caution:

Using the comma between two independent clauses (sentences that can stand on their own) causes a *comma splice*. Stylistically this is acceptable to some, though others frown upon it, opting instead to use a period.

For example:

> **Comma splice:** He doubled back, the dog was waiting.

Vs.

> **Correct form:** He doubled back. The dog was waiting.

CLAUSES

Independent Clauses are sentences that stand alone.

> **For example:** The boy was afraid.

Dependent Clauses cannot stand alone.

> **For example:** Because the boy was afraid (it needs more information, correct? It's dependent.)

Of course it must result in something else.

> e.g.: Because the boy was afraid, he ran.

You can fix comma splices by adding a semicolon or a period. Be careful, however, semicolons quickly become noticeable and can drag a reader out of the story if they are used in excess.

Even though it causes a comma splice, if you *cannot* use a period, use a comma to separate related, independent clauses.

SEMICOLON

No. Just…don't. Don't touch it. Don't fiddle with it. You will probably end up overusing it and ruining your book. Leave it alone.

For the record, the semicolon's function is not all that diverse. One way it is used is to join two independent clauses that are related.

For example:

> The sun set early; a storm was coming.

To reiterate: the overuse of the semicolon can take a reader out of the story. In fact, it is very easy for a reader to spot them again and again and again.

Stylistically, the sentence above could pass even with a comma splice:

>The sun set early, a storm was coming.

Or a period:

>The sun set early. A storm was coming.

So while semicolons are useful, the gain hardly outweighs the risk and therefore, unless you are more comfortable with grammar overall, it may be best just to leave it alone for now.

So…don't touch it. At. All.

I mean it….

ELLIPSES

You will certainly overuse these, too. Try to cut back on them by using dialogue tags to help show hesitation. Ellipses consist of three dots in a row for ongoing dialogue; four dots in a row for dialogue that tapers off and ends. They are meant for omissions for quotes but many authors use them to show trepidation or doubt. You will often see them with a space before and after the three dots—even a space before the fourth dot.

> "Hello … Mary." John inched closer. "… You look hungry … ."

Whenever you look for a 'how to' on ellipses, you are likely to find different information each time. It boils down to a matter of style in the end. The above example was the most academic. For a nonfiction book such as this one, I recommend the above approach. For your *novel*, however, I am against it. Even as I write this, my software is trying to remove the space before the fourth dot.

The trouble with these spaces is that it causes a lot of problems when you are formatting a book. The ellipses before the word 'You' should be on the same line. Word processors won't do that automatically in this case. Here is one way of using them that fixes all formatting errors. The easiest way to make sure it formats well both on the digital version and the paperback is to remove those extra spaces (this method will not add or take away from your word count).

Recommendation: no spaces.

> "How…how are you, Mary?" he asked.
> Mary clutched the urn close. "I'm fine, I guess…."

Usually there is no comma after the third dot, and now look at it with no spaces. The letter after the ellipse in a quote is lowercase.

> "I'd like to see him…" **she** whispered, choking back a sob. "**If** it's okay…."

or

> "I'd like to see him…" [3 dots] **she** whispered, choking back a sob, "if it's okay."

Compare this to a sentence without a dialogue tag.

> "I'd like to see him…." [4 dots] **She** paused to catch her breath. Finally, she said, "If that's okay."

You will notice that the word after the three dots is lower case while the word after the four dots is capitalized. An ellipsis is three dots. The fourth dot indicates an end (a period). Whatever you decide, *be consistent*. Remember that style is up to the author.

PERIOD

The period—a full stop—is a great tool for emphasis. Nothing quite wakes a reader up like slamming on the brakes. It's great for conveying anger or an adamant stance.

> Hands on her hips, his mother said, "No. You're not going. I repeat: You. Are. Not. Going."

Use it in exposition as well.

> Twenty years at this factory without a day off. Not. Even. One. Mark had nothing to show for his dedication.

As with all punctuation that stands out, use it sparingly.

APOSTROPHE

In school most of us learn to indicate possession using **apostrophe s** after a word without **s**, while **s apostrophe** came with plurals. What about names ending in **s** such as James?

Possession:

This is John**'s** car.

This is Jame**s's** car. ("This is James' car," is also acceptable.)

This is the people**'s** car.

These are our wive**s'** cars.

This is someone else**'s** car.

This is the octopu**s'** car.

These are the octopuse**s'** cars.

These are the mice**'s** cars.

This is the FBI**'s** car.

Note some biblical exceptions:

Jesus'

Moses'

Dates:

'80s cars, '80s music

1990's music

the 1990s

Missing Letters:

I don't need your stinkin' money.

ENDNOTES

No.

FOOTNOTES

Don't you *dare*….

A novel is for escape, if the information is so plentiful that people need to keep notes…that's a bad sign.

DASHES

The em dash (or en dash) is not a hyphen; it is longer. In MS Word, for example, two hyphens (--) will change to an em dash if you do not include spaces.

There are three functions of an em dash: afterthought, interruption, and introduction of information.

Afterthought

> She liked him well enough—but what a jerk.
>
> "One cannot live on bread alone—or so I hear."

An interruption

> My boss—Roger—smells like cabbage.
>
> That left only the three of them—Ricky, Bobby, and Tam—to fend alone. They didn't stand a chance.

Show a specific explanation

> James goes to Philadelphia for one reason—he loves the food.
>
> "You know. There's a *word* for people like you— peasant."
>
> She loved him for his one true talent—he could sing.

CAPITALIZATION

Other than capitalizing names and place names, here are some other examples where something usually lowercased would need capitalization.

Do you know that my **mother** is very kind?

Vs.

Do you know that **Mother** is very kind?

Capitalize when calling someone by a title.

If you create any new organizations or race of people, capitalize them.

The **Sarili** people were friendly and kind.

Emphasis:

When making emphasis on a word, rather than capitalize, italicize the word in question.

We *really* need to get a gun.

Also, use the period to stress the words more.

Mary pulled the curtains. "We *really* need to get a gun. Now."

"A *gun*? Is that really necessary?" Roger asked.

"There are zombies at our doorstep, Roger. We. Need. A. Gun."

Caution:

Using parentheses ( ) in creative writing narration is frowned upon. Likewise, use exclamation marks in dialogue *only*.

There are of course much more grammar points to learn. A pure grammar book is essential for a writer. You do not have to read it cover to cover and memorize it, but you will need it for quick references.

NUMBERS

Numbers should always be spelled out in creative writing.

They married **five** years ago and settled down shortly after.

A year from now, **two hundred years** from now, their love would still burn strong. Brandi, **thirty-five**, and Jordan, **twenty-six**, turned heads no matter where they went.

Their **eight-year-old** daughter hurried down the stairs. Tomorrow, she would be **nine years old**.

EXCLAMATION MARK

I cannot stress enough caution in using this. This little mark (!) is well-loved by many authors and hated *bitterly* by nearly every reader known to man. Some say an author is allowed *one* exclamation mark per 90,000 words. That's being generous. If you must use it, keep it in dialogue only, not in exposition (the narration itself).

Doubling it (!!) does not make it stronger, it only doubles its wretchedness. While it is a good tool, its abuse (and overuse) can lead to disaster. Limit yourself to a few per *book* (in dialogue only).

Your scene should be so well-painted that tension is already established without the benefit of this mark. If this mark is necessary, revisit your chapter. Ratchet up the tension elsewhere—either in the setting or the consequences.

I humbly invite you to challenge yourself by summoning this mark with great reluctance. Consider the use of the exclamation mark as an act of desperation. From this moment forward, 'the *desperation mark*' is equivalent to marrying your ninety-eight-year-old brother-uncle on his deathbed rather than dying alone.

Resolve to die alone…please.

2-2. STYLE & SYNTAX

This might be one of the most lax areas…to a point. Style is up to the author. Ultimately, it'll always be up to the author. But there are grammar rules in place.

Some would argue many successful authors break those rules—some break them rather well—and it adds to their style. I agree. However, it's important to learn those rules before you break them.

RULES & SUGGESTIONS

Here are a few rules you might have heard that are still practiced by many.

- reduce your adverbs

- keep the sentences short (to avoid run-ons and to keep the pace quick)

- don't start sentences with 'and' or 'but'

- don't break the fourth wall (see **content editing**)

- reduce your use of sentences starting with the **present participle** (e.g., Stumbling, she made her way through the crowd). 'Stumbling' uses the present participle, verb+ing. Not to be confused with **gerunds**: E.g., *Painting houses is his job.* 'Painting' is now a verb turned noun—it's a gerund. Gerunds do not pose a problem.

- *don't start consecutive paragraphs with the same letter*

- *don't start consecutive sentences with the same word*

- don't start a sentence with 'it'

- don't end a sentence with a preposition (on, to, at, by)

- don't use parenthesis e.g., ( )

- *don't use exclamation marks outside of dialogue*

- use italics to show emphasis rather than uppercase.

- don't use the same pattern on consecutive sentences. For example: Biting her nails, she sat down. Pulling a bowl close, she made her breakfast. Talking with her mouth full, she said, "Isn't this type of pattern rather off-putting?"

I've italicized the ones I think are the most important to consider using.

ORDER & SEQUENCE

This is one that is not always easy to catch, but it's worth looking out for. Often times, a *reaction* is presented before an *action*.

> Tears swelled in Mary's eyes when she saw him waiting for her by the door.

At first glance, there's nothing really wrong with this. However, for greater impact, consider showing the *action* first then the *reaction*.

Consider:

> There he stood, waiting at her door. Tears swelled in her eyes. One fell, and then another.

Allow the reader to experience the action with the character.

OVER-TELLING

Over-telling occurs when the author is too detailed in each and every aspect of the characters' movement. Giving the reader this information is very important—the reader wants it. However, there is such a thing as *too much*.

Here's an example.

> She crossed the room and opened the window. From here the dogs playing in the distance were easy to make out.
>
> One pup tumbled over. It stood up again. It fell over again.
>
> She closed the window. After latching it, she sat down in her chair and brought her feet up.

These details bring your scene to life and are well-appreciated, but was each and every part necessary? To a point some weren't.

Consider:

> She crossed the room and opened the window. Two dogs played in the distance.
>
> One pup tumbled over and over.
>
> After latching the window, she sat down in her chair and brought her feet up.

Not each and every single aspect of the scene is necessary. Say as much as you can with the fewest words possible. If you can afford to cut something without losing content, always *cut*.

Other examples of over-telling include:

He stood up. (Standing means to go up unless we indicate otherwise.)

→ He stood.

She shrugged her shoulders. (Rarely do we shrug another body part other than shoulders.)

→ She shrugged.

She blinked her eyes. (We cannot blink other body parts; therefore 'her eyes' is unnecessary.)

→ She blinked.

REPETITION, REPETITION (OH, AND LEST WE FORGET…REPETITION)

Repetition is hard to see while you are writing. We tend to reach for the fastest and easiest words that come to mind, not realizing we've just used them in such close proximity that they stand out.

Example:

> He looked out the window. The first snow of the year was beautiful as usual. It looked like diamonds shimmering in the warm sunlight.
>
> "Hey," a voice called.
>
> He looked back to see who.
>
> "Come see this. It looks amazing."

Did you notice the repetition by chance? The word 'look' was used four times. Two or more in close proximity is too much. Go through your work slowly and find these repetitive actions, words, or gestures. Change them.

Suggestion:

> Outside the window the first snow of the year shimmered like diamonds in the warm sunlight—beautiful as usual.
>
> "Hey," a voice called.
>
> He looked back to see who.
>
> "Come see this. It's amazing."

Two or more is too much. Rather than 'look,' he 'glanced back,' 'swung around,' etc. etc. would have worked well (as well. Just kidding) also.

Another form of repetition:

Be mindful when repeating *information* that is important to the story. Yes, a reader needs a reminder from time to time about something you hope to use later on. Surprisingly, not many reminders are necessary. For some reason, we are able to retain small details well as we read. A reminder every few **chapters** is acceptable, but not every chapter, and not too often—especially when the clump of information is worded similarly.

Patterns start to stand out. While some patterns are good, others can interrupt the flow of your story. This is another reason excessive adverbs become a problem. We start to notice them more and more because their endings are all 'ly.'

So cut back on the repetition. It can quickly wear on your reader's patience.

Equally, remember to foreshadow. A surprise that has never been mentioned, yet suddenly 'jumps' out at a reader, can leave one feeling betrayed and confused. Much like a 'surprise' gift from your cat…in the form of a mangled dead rat on your pillow, a sudden 'plot twist' might have been well-intended…but that's not how it was received.

You want to entice your audience, not compel them to fling their e-reader across the room. Foreshadow.

FILTER WORDS

Filter words are words that filter emotion or action through a character before it reaches the reader. There's nothing wrong with them sporadically, but reducing them can open up a lot more possibilities. Filter words include, but aren't limited to: she saw, she smelled, she knew, she felt, she heard.

These words are somewhat *telling* rather than *showing*. They were touched on earlier but here is yet another example of them.

Filtered:

I heard drums sound from the north. I knew that meant war.

Unfiltered:

Drums sounded from the north. That meant war.

Filtered:

He felt the cat rub against his leg. Reaching down, he stroked it.

Unfiltered:

The cat rubbed against his leg. Reaching down, he stroked it. (He reached down and stroked it.)

Filtered:

She saw the horses charging toward her.

Unfiltered:

The horses charged toward her.

Filtered:

His hands felt coarse against her skin as it traveled up her body.

Unfiltered:

> His coarse hands traveled up her body. Her skin
> tingled.

Rather than filter these actions through the character, give
them to the reader directly. This method still maintains the
POV (Point of View) and brings a greater impact to the
situation.

Don't forget: action first *then* reaction.

RUN-ONS

Long sentences might feel justified. They might even feel
beautiful and artistic.

No.

In reality, they are exhausting. A reader must try to digest all
those words and keep them in mind. Shorter sentences make
for a cleaner, crisper read.

> He took her by the hand, crossed the park, and
> showed her where he hoped to marry her one day—
> if only she would give him that chance, the chance
> of a lifetime, the one thing he wanted.

This sentence is a lot to take in. It's so long that it looks like a paragraph. Cutting it up—breaking that run-on—can make it stronger and easier to read.

Suggestion:

He took her by the hand and led her across the park. Here, by the flowerbed, is where he hoped to marry her one day.

Their eyes met. If only she would give him that chance, the chance of a lifetime—the one thing he wanted.

2-3. SUBJECT-VERB AGREEMENT

Subject-verb agreement means that the verb tense matches the subject. Smaller sentences are very easy to construct correctly.

> Leroy is the strongest.

But once the sentences get longer and longer, the agreement gets tricky.

> Leroy who lives in that house **is** the strongest.

> Leroy who lives in that house and fights foreclosure at every turn despite the odds **is** the strongest.

Be mindful of these others as well. Though they can be confusing, it's important to remember the subject is singular, therefore so is the verb.

> Each of them tries to open the door.

Neither of them wants to open the door.

Any one of them who tries to open the door will fail.

None of these keys opens the door.

Either of them opens the door.

When using *and* to join two subjects, then the verb is plural.

James and Marcus play baseball every Sunday.

However, when joining two things using *or*, *nor*, *as well as*, *plus*, *together with*, and *along with*, the verb is singular.

James, together with Marcus, plays baseball every Sunday.

James, along with Marcus, plays baseball every Sunday.

Neither James nor Marcus plays baseball every Sunday.

Either James or Marcus is expected to play baseball every Sunday.

James, plus Marcus, plays baseball every Sunday.

Be mindful of your pronouns matching as well.

This is incorrect:

> Anyone can befriend dragons, if **they** try hard enough.

Anyone is singular, therefore, that pronoun must be singular as well.

This is correct:

> Anyone can befriend dragons if **he** tries hard enough.

> Anyone can befriend dragons if **she tries** hard enough.

> Anyone can befriend dragons if **he/she** tries hard enough.

> All **people** can befriend dragons if **they** try hard enough.

ASHLYN FORGE

2-4. EASILY CONFUSED WORDS

One of the most basic yet potentially embarrassing issues in writing is misused words. They sound the same, and sometimes their use is very similar. But here are some words to keep in mind and how they are used.

BARE VS. BEAR

Bare: **adjective/verb** means not covered. Naked. It also means 'open to view,' for example:

> She laid all my secrets bare.

It also means 'no higher unit.'

For example:

> Bring just the bare necessities.

Just tell me the bare facts.

Touching bare wires is a bad idea.

When they got home, the house was bare—absolutely empty.

Now compare it to **bear** which means to *endure, bring fruit,* and *keep.*

The tree didn't bear fruit and the woman to tend it didn't bear offspring.

His weak threats were hard to bear in mind.

I'm so sorry for missing the deadline. Please bear with me.

The burden of this fight was hard to bear.

AFFECT VS. EFFECT

The use of these words is very difficult for many. Think of 'affection' and 'special effects.'

Affect has to do with emotion. The word also means influence.

Your threats don't affect me.

Compared to Effect which means result:

Listening to that song didn't have any effect on him.

He needed more tablets to get the same effect.

The effects were lackluster.

LIE VS. LAY

The words 'lie down' and 'lay eggs' should put these two into perspective.

Here are some examples that should help. Your understanding of these two might never be perfect, but hopefully the basic uses will stick. Don't fret too much, though, the average reader doesn't know either. It's the pedants you want to dance around. Or perhaps you'd like the bragging rights yourself.

Please keep in mind most spellcheckers can help you select the right one.

Lie → Lay → Lain (rest horizontally, inactive, helpless, sex, direction)

He decided to lie in wait.

Guilt lies heavy on him.

The city lies west.

His anger lies **with** his mother and sister.

The choice lies with her.

Lay → Laid → Laid (to put, to burden)

He couldn't follow through on his well-laid plans.

The army marches through and lays waste the kingdom.

WET VS. WHET

Wet: means consisting of water.

In the shower, she wet her hair.

Whet: means to sharpen or stimulate with excitement.

The blacksmith whet the knife.

Talk like that whet his appetite for a fight.

PEAK/ PEEK/ PIQUE

Peak means the very height.

We made it to the mountain peak.

Peek means to look at someone secretly.

She peeked through the window curtains.

Pique means a sudden feeling.

The news of the new position opening up piqued his interest.

PEACE VS. PIECE

"Speak now or forever hold your **peace**," the priest said, but Frank kept quiet. This was no longer his fight—he'd already said his **piece**.

Confusion isn't always limited to verbs. It happens to the best of us when writing a draft quickly; some **pronouns** get confused. Here are some basic ones that are easy to find and fix. Ignoring them can lead a reader to lose faith in your writing so be careful.

THEY'RE / THEIR / THERE

They're = They are

They're friends.

They're all lovely flowers. Thank you.

Their = possessive pronoun

It's their turn to drive the carpool.

I hope their dog hasn't done his business on the lawn again.

That's their daughter. You stay away from her.

There = location, it is also a word that introduces a sentence 'there is, there are'

There are ten zombies at our doorstep. They didn't bring mac and cheese, either.

There are some things we need to discuss before going out there to all hell on earth.

Are there any guns out there?

Park over there.

YOUR / YOU'RE

Your = possessive pronoun

Your name's Earl Lee? Is there a joke behind that?

I don't like your tone.

You're = you are

Earl Lee? Really? You're kidding, right? Oh wow, you're not. S—sorry. I shouldn't have laughed so loud.

You're so much taller than I expected. Smellier, too.

IT'S / ITS

It's = it is

It's nice to meet you.

Look outside! It's lovely out.

It's about time you left. Go home, jerk.

Its = possessive pronoun

Its black hair dripped with blood.

Its wide eyes, raw and red, put me in the mind of a disenchanted figure—lost and afraid.

Is this your pet? What's its name?

2-5. TRIMMING THE FAT

This is by far one of the hardest steps you will have to take. There will be other difficult ones, but it starts with this.

Trimming—cutting out things you don't need. People often describe it as 'killing your darlings.' That is a true statement, but you're not ready for the total killing yet. With this, you're going to make some painful cuts that'll leave your darlings writhing in agony as they bleed out. And as they whine and scream at you for mercy, you're going to ignore them, and keep *right* on hacking! You have to. It's for your own good— and theirs as well.

You need to be as objective as you can, so it's really recommended you let the piece sit for a number of months to a year or more before attempting this. Give yourself some time to forget your story before you read it again.

I'll wait....

...

Finished? Okay, welcome back. I know it's been about three or four months (*at least*) but let's continue.

The first cut is the excess. If you have a dialogue tag followed by an action, consider cutting out the dialogue tag (if the paragraph won't suffer).

"Get up!" John said, jumping to his feet.

Turns into...

John jumped to his feet. "Get up!"

If you were good with using proper dialogue tags while maintaining only one person per paragraph then this trim should be easy.

Also:

John nodded and said, "Sure."

Turns into...

John nodded. "Sure."

The second cut involves information. Too often we over-tell, over-write. Each chapter has a focus, has a purpose. From start to finish, it must *always* tie into the plot. So cut away anything that does not tie into it.

Lengthy backstory? No one cares. Save it for another chapter when the reader is emotionally invested. Need to foreshadow? You only get one sentence to hint—two tops.

If you don't use the information somewhere else in the book later on, *cut* it. If the information focuses on a person or object you never follow up on in the book? *Cut it.*

The third cut is adverbs. Adverbs are words that end in 'ly.' E.g., *quickly*, *quietly* etc. These are adjectives that describe a verb. Adverbs rob you of a great opportunity to flesh out your writing. It's telling at its worst for the most part.

"Get out here!" John said angrily.

In this one line (containing a double sin: adverb *and* desperation mark—exclamation mark), the author tells us how John feels. Therefore there's no reason for the author to emphasize it in other ways. The exclamation mark can stay if you're terribly attached to it, but not both.

If using the exclamation mark equates to marrying your brother-uncle, then having both that mark *and* an adverb would be marrying the man while your hand hovers over the plug to his life-support, ready to disconnect him after the ink dries on his will. It's overkill.

Adverbs are a danger to one very important aspect: setting the mood.

Other times it's the opposite; the author sets the mood but uses adverbs and the information is hammered away inadvertently.

Take John above. Depending on what's going on, the reader can feel the tension. The exclamation point shows emotion. There hardly seems a reason to doubt that he's angry.

Depending on the scene and how well you paint it, adverbs are often unnecessary. Most can be removed without taking away anything from the tone or narrative and if they are necessary then consider fleshing out the scene better.

Paint your scene and remove adverbs.

Here is an example:

> Beep. Pop. Buzz. Whish. A room so active with sound still seemed dead within. Outside, birds flew, people laughed, children fell down and bruised their knees. The world lived—the world thrived as it should but Maggie couldn't help but hate each and every one of them.
>
> In her sixty-six years, she had never felt so numb. That hollowed chasm where her heart should have been only grew when she found the courage to focus on her daughter, Sue. The various machines that kept Sue breathing held Maggie's gaze for far too long.

The doctor said something, but Maggie didn't hear.

"Sorry?" Maggie asked (absentmindedly).

"I'm sorry ma'am. There's nothing more we can do."

'Nothing more.' The jerk said it ~~so calmly. To him,~~ [as if] Sue was just another nameless faceless patient once the day was out. He didn't scream it. He didn't sob it. He didn't give Maggie's daughter even an iota of emotion. He gave Sue *nothing* she deserved.

Maggie swallowed down her rebuttal and forced a smile. "I see," she said (bitterly).

As you can see, the adverbs can be cut out. There's no need to go out of your way to cut out each and every adverb. Adverbs aren't terrible, but they are easy to grab. Too many of them can pose a real problem. Rather than adverbs, try reaching for strong verbs.

He pulled quickly. → he grabbed, he yanked, he snatched, he dragged, etc.

She ran quickly. → she raced, she dashed, etc.

He whispered nervously, "Did you see that monster?" → He whispered, "Did—did you see that monster?"

Please see the 'Showing vs. Telling' area below for more information.

The fourth cut is 'filter words.' As mentioned before, these are words that filter emotion through the character rather than directly to the reader. They, too, weaken your writing and rob you and your reader of a more dynamic narration.

Filter words include but are not limited to: he knew, he saw, he heard, he felt, and he smelled, etc.

For example:

He smelled burning bodies.

This sensation is filtered.

Consider:

Ash from burning bodies hung on the breeze.

e.g.,

She saw a rattle snake rise from the grass, ready to strike.

Consider:

A rattle snake rose from the grass, ready to strike.

e.g.,

> The knife fell. He felt it rip through his shoe.

Consider:

> The knife fell. It ripped through his shoe.

e.g.,

> He felt the cold wind blow. He shivered.

Consider:

> The cold wind blew. He shivered.

The fifth cut is the word 'was.' It is nearly *impossible* to write a book without the word *was*. And yet, it's still troublesome when you have a lot of instances of 'was.' *Was* is sometimes indicative of an upcoming data-dump. Other instances might show up along with passive voice: *The ball **was taken** from his hand.* Find all your 'was' sentences and double check them.

Look out for: was+verb-ing

> He was eating a sandwich as Trevor walked in.

Consider:

> He sat eating a sandwich as Trevor walked in.

Or:

> He ate a sandwich as Trevor walked in.

Was+verb-ing states movement that took place (or started) beforehand. While that's not terrible, it can make the reader feel as though they are late to the action. Put the scene in the here and now.

One last cut to consider is 'that.' This removal is optional.

Consider:

> "She said **that** it's too late and **that** you should come back tomorrow."

> Vs.

> "She said it's too late and you should come back tomorrow."

Consider:

> "I didn't know **that** he was back in town."

> Vs.

> "I didn't know he was back in town."

Caution: While you can remove 'that' after a verb, you cannot remove it from the verbs **shout** or **reply**. You also should not remove it after a noun. "I am of the opinion that diamonds are forever." Feel free to remove it after adjectives: "I'm so glad that you called." → "I'm so glad you called."

3. Content Editing

This section will help you edit your content for free. Fortunately, this is one area that can be done without cost but it does take some work.

Warning: the <u>only</u> way this will work is if you go into this thinking your draft is horrible.

Too often, authors are in love with their stories; their characters; their *masterpiece*. While you should ultimately love what you've written and be proud of the accomplishment of finishing a draft (many will never get this far), you *need* to put your ego on hold and allow others to step on your baby, relentlessly.

Say it. Say, "I need help. This draft is hideous."

Have you said it? Good. Now take this kid out and let others bash it in the face until it's pretty.

Ready? Okay. Let's talk about your state of mind. This is no joke; you really have to psych yourself up.

When you hire a development editor or a content editor, his/her job is to take your piece apart and make it work. This means bringing a bat against your ego. *And* you have to pay him!

Repeat. A content editor will likely leave your manuscript bleeding red ink, ruining most of your self-confidence with it (the good editors)…*and* you have to pay!

This is something you can get for free…sometimes.

Caution: If you use an editor, this content edit should occur *first* then the line edit. The reason being that in content edits, you have to cut or add to the piece. If you have polished the grammar, you'll need to do it all over again because it has changed. If you self-edit mostly, do this bit second, however.

Also, keep in mind that a professional editor is of course faster in helping you with this area. They know how a story *should* develop. They know of bad habits to look out for. They know what it takes to make a good solid story (usually), so by going it alone, this responsibility is now yours. Go slow, and be thorough.

3-1. POINT OF VIEW (POV)

Point of view means *how* we see the world the author is creating. When you write, you select whether to use:

- first person present

- first person past

- second person

- third person present

- third person past

- omniscient

First person is a popular point of view to use. This is depicted with the reader being inside the head of one character. It's generally a safe POV since we are limited to what we can know and see. Unfortunately, it can also lead to long (often ineffective) monologues, background stories, data dumps, and sentences after sentences of 'I.'

There are two tenses to choose from: **first person past**, or **first person present**.

First person past looks like this.

> I **ran** my fingers down his back.

First person present looks like this.

> I **run** my fingers down his back.

The present tense is a bit harder to keep but whichever you decide on, *commit* to it. Nothing is more painful than going through a 60,000 word manuscript to change each and every tense.

Second person is a bit rare. It's not every day that you'll encounter it. Rather than use *I* it uses *you*.

> You run your hands down his back.

The third person POV is equally as common as the first person. **Third person past** tense is rather popular.

Third person past looks something like this.

> He raced down the street.

Third person present looks like this.

He races down the street.

Whether you use first or third, please keep in mind that third person doesn't have to be distant. You can still get very close to the characters if you use third person limited. **Third person limited** is when you stick close to one person's point of view, including their emotions.

Here is an example.

> John caught the railing before he fell. He held on so tight his arms burned. Should he fall from this height, he would be walking with a limp for the rest of his life—if he was lucky. For the first time in his thirty-five years, he almost cried out for his mother.
>
> *Not that she'd come even if I called*, he thought.

I saved the **omniscient** POV for last because it is the most problematic. It is the POV everyone *thinks* they are using, but they really aren't. This POV is very difficult to do well—it's not impossible, just difficult. The biggest problem with attempting to use this POV is that it can quickly lead to *head-hopping* which is a big no-no.

WHAT IS HEAD-HOPPING?

It's when a scene has multiple POVs (view points and emotions) and thoughts. The idea is to be all-knowing. That sometimes goes as far as allowing the reader access to knowledge not granted to any of the characters.

Switching POV mid-scene or through the scene is very jarring. If you have to switch POV, do so at a different scene, or in a different chapter.

Head-hopping might seem innocent enough while you are writing, but as a reader, it can cause a whiplash effect.

THE DANGERS OF HEAD-HOPPING

Consider this passage.

Jeremy tried to shake Jasmine awake. "Get up!" he cried, his voice cracking. Her body flopped below his grip. With the raiders closing in, the alarm should have woken her.

Below the thin covers, Jasmine feigned sleep. She refused to participate in any ritual that might take the life of another human being. As badly as she wanted to tell Jeremy this, she resisted.

Bill swung the door open and busted in. His back hunched, he marched over to them and grunted. "They've come," he said, a grave frown etched on his bearded face. "It's time we bleed all the pigs in preparation for the ceremony. Bring the witch." Bill shook his head as he walked out, still bitter that he was forced to allow a woman into his chambers.

If throughout this entire passage, none of this seems out of place to you, chances are, you're guilty of head-hopping. Tsk, tsk, tsk.

Most people argue it's fairly common now and there is nothing wrong with it, many disagree. If I may make a brief argument as to why it's not a good idea to head-hop. Other than the fact that it's said to be frowned upon in the publishing world, it's also ineffective storytelling.

When we take on a POV, we are wearing a character like an extra layer of skin (ew, I know, but hang in there). Thus we are seeing this new world through their eyes, as if the skull is hollowed out and we are staring through them. Poke. Poke (stop cringing, this is for your own good).

Let's first start with Jeremy. We are supposed to feel his apprehension. We're supposed to feel how tense he is and how panicked he might feel. He has this seemingly unconscious woman to deal with and raiders are coming. We are now wearing him like a suit (shh, just let the image come into your head, don't fight it), and we are in the story.

Then we *shift* over to Jasmine, and now we have to share *her* reluctance. Thus we've dropped the tension Jeremy felt—we shed him—and we are now thrown into a new set of emotions to experience; a whole new body. She's being petty or hoping to sabotage them, etc. etc. so her motivations change. Sure this squishy, new body's warm, but the perspective is gone. It's a whole new body (stop touching it) and the reader has to start over emotionally.

Then finally Bill…we are now angry because Bill is angry. All these arrays of emotions in a small amount of time. The spell is broken and we are thrown out of the story at this point.

There are better ways to show the reader *all* of these emotions while still maintaining *one* point of view.

HOW DO WE FIX IT?

Choose the strongest character. Stay in that character's skull and tell us what they know. Without using filter words, get all of that across.

Observe (Jeremy's) thoughts are written in italics.

Jeremy tried to shake Jasmine awake. "Get up!" he cried, his voice shaky. Her body flopped below his grip. With the raiders closing in, the alarm should have woken her.

Her eyes flicked open for a moment below the thin covers. Jasmine feigned sleep. That realization changed Jeremy's world. At a time like this, when everyone needed them, she refused to participate in the ritual.

He tried to make sense of it. *Is she reluctant because it will cost us the life of another human being?* Jeremy thought. An hour prior, she had seemed intent on telling Jeremy something, her lips had twitched. *She had no reason to resist. She could have told me.*

Heavy footsteps drew his focus.

Bill swung the door open and busted in. His back hunched, he marched over to them and grunted. "They've come," he said, a grave frown etched on his bearded face. "It's time we bleed the pigs in preparation for the ceremony. Bring the witch." Bill gave Jasmine's seemingly lifeless frame a long stare.

He's still bitter that he was forced to allow a woman into his chambers. What a petty issue to think about at a time like this! Jeremy thought.

Yes the story got a bit longer, but we could wear Jeremy's flesh a bit better (seriously…yuck). We are limited to his eyes but there are other ways to convey it while keeping the tension or the mood you've set.

Instead of thoughts, dialogue would have worked easily as well. If an author employs head-hopping, it is somewhat like whiplash. *One POV* then *whoosh*, another, then *whoosh* another.

Imagine if you will: happy character → sad character → apathetic → evil → righteous, etc., etc., etc. It's exhausting.

These are all the emotions we get dragged through as we read. Paint the picture and consider lopping off and claiming one head, and one head only, so that you can wriggle your way into that body and ride that meat suit into this *charming* new world.

3-2. YOUR FIRST CHAPTER

First chapters are difficult, so difficult in fact that you're likely to write this chapter last. Don't worry if your first chapter doesn't shine, but worry if your beta readers *cannot* read past your first chapter.

Each chapter is like a mini book. There is build up, a high point, then a cliff-hanger ending or a short resolution. That cliff-hanger will help carry your reader on to the following chapters.

With so many books released daily, it's imperative that your first chapter be as smooth as possible.

THINGS TO REMEMBER

- **Don't introduce a lot of characters in the first chapter.** Any character you give a name to, you essentially introduce (even characters not yet present in the scene). Introduce as few characters as you can—two, *maybe* three.

75

- **Nobody cares about your characters.** *Don't* go into lengthy backstories about their feelings or an experience that doesn't relate to the here and now. Once a reader gets interested in your characters and your world, they will care about what happens to them. But in the beginning, unless you hit a very specific nerve close to home (e.g., cancer patient and the reader has experience with cancer in the family) chances are, the reader won't feel much emotional attachment to your character.

- **Don't give large blocks of text (exposition), then clumps of dialogue, then long blocks of text again.**

- **Avoid prologues if you can.** All that information that the prologue conveys should be peppered throughout the first chapter.

- **Give your character movement.** Make them *do* something. Avoid having your character simply remaining dormant, daydreaming, or staring out a window. *Move* that character.

- **Give your character a clear conflict (a problem) to overcome.**

- **Don't change scenes in the first chapter if you can help it.** It's important to hold your reader's attention for as long as possible.

- **Introduce your character's personality and hardships through his/her reactions to their everyday life.** Don't state it. *Show it.*

- **Don't mention anything you don't plan to follow up on.**

- **Don't spend too much time on description.** Give enough, but not to the point where you leave the reader simply looking at the scenery and nothing more.

A FIRST CHAPTER IS LIKE A FIRST DATE

Readers sit down with your book. They're nervous, they are excited, they are maybe a bit cautious, too. They open it. The first line is a turn off. It started with a cliché waking up scene, perhaps. The "What's your sign" of the literature world. Your book just said, "I'm a boring person." Okay, that's a bad start. So choose your opener and make sure it reflects the chapter—maybe even the book.

But even with a bad opener, they might keep going. You can still get lucky.

A lot of people *start* their first chapters well, but then as the date gets comfortable and the reader gets interested, suddenly your book goes into a lengthy back story about a character not present or a great deal of exposition. And as your book is going on and on about that, no dialogue, no showing, no motion, your reader gets bored, and starts looking around for someone else to date for the night.

"Oh, but it's important to the story!" you say. Yes, but you don't go on a first date and start talking about how your dog died and you never got over it, when the scene opens with a crime taking place instead!

STAY ON TOPIC

If the story is talking about a character's personal life, don't mention a new topic in great length. Stay on topic.

Daddy issues? Save it. No personal life? Save it. You get *one* line to hint at these new topics. *One*, and stay on topic. If you open up with a chase, don't do a mini flashback about what happened *before* the chase. Stay on topic. And *stay* in the here and now.

e.g., this is a 'no-no'

Barry caught the next baseball before it struck him in the face. The crowd fell silent. At that speed, catching a ball barehanded should have hurt. Everyone stared at him as if he should react with less calm.

Handing the baseball over to the catcher, he tried to smile under his over-sized batting helmet. He gripped the bat again and took a wide stance.

"Let's go," he said.

He'd always been like that. He could burn his hands and not feel any pain. When he was five years old he nearly drowned in a pond. His uncle jumped in and swam to save him. Ever since that time he'd known he was different. Throughout his life, he'd had to hide his strange nature. Sometimes he'd forget to act normal. When he'd go into work and burn his hand on the fryer by mistake. Or times when he was getting an injection and moved around without thinking.

Maybe that's why he didn't have a girlfriend. It'd be hard to explain to a woman why he'd always have bruises on his body from not being careful. He wanted a girlfriend though, it was lonely being in high school without any close friends.

Barry, Barry, Barry! Did your reader (date) need all that dumped on him/her before the salad even arrived?

Mini-data-dumps and long blocks of text with little dialogue aren't all that effective—especially when we get carried away to when the character was five years old. Why should the reader care?

Suggestion:

Barry caught the next baseball before it struck him in the face. The crowd fell silent. At that speed, catching a ball barehanded should have hurt. Everyone stared at him as if he should react with less calm.

Handing the baseball over to the catcher, he tried to smile under his over-sized batting helmet. He gripped the bat again and took a wide stance.

"Let's go," he said, chalking this up to yet another inexplicable bruise to add to all the others.

When he thought of the fact that his family no longer asked and he had no girl to explain himself to, he swung with all his might.

"Strike!" The umpire announced.

Two more balls flew his way and he struck out miserably. His body might not feel pain, but his pride definitely took a hit.

He lumbered back to the dugout, all eyes on him. The first time he'd seen those expressions, he was five and he nearly drowned. The other players now wore the same look of confusion and worry his uncle had after dragging his very alive body from that water. He'd been a freak back then, too.

Throughout his life, he'd had to hide his strange nature. Sometimes he'd forget to act normal. Today he'd messed up big time. This wasn't like work where he'd burn his hand on the fryer by mistake and could hide it. People had seen.

"Another great year of high school, here I come," he grumbled as he flopped down on the bench. Other players inched further away from him.

Compare the two compositions. The first with the isolated data-dumps had a lot of exposition clumped together. Your book was going on and on.

The second example spread it out between dialogue and movement. Stay in the here and now. Compare now to past events, but don't go into a mini-flashback where you take the reader back in time. The reader barely knows your book. Don't try to shove them into a tinted van (time machine) within the first three minutes. They are going to resist.

ALSO, AVOID THE SWITCH-A-ROO

This occurs when the chapter opens with one character and switches to a new character halfway. So basically your date sits down and tries to get comfortable. Your second character comes by and sits and starts to talk while the first character isn't involved. Suddenly that first character is just gone and a new one is there instead. It's jarring. (She's turning on her GPS tracking app and texting your profile to her family and friends in case she goes missing.)

Now your date's chewing on some lettuce, feeling a bit abandoned and wondering why he/she should care about this new character. No connection between the two characters, just a brand new character out of nowhere. One character just stood up and another one sat down. So whatever inkling of emotional investment a reader might have felt with character one, is now wiped away. She's not taking your book home tonight. She's never going to call.

There are many different scenarios for what makes a lousy date. Imagine your characters as real, imagine your reader as being on a date, and keep it interesting.

Don't leave your character alone delving into his/her thoughts for too long. Give the reader information by *showing* it unfold. You can hint at things, but stay focused. You want your reader to follow you home to chapter two, not dawdle at the doorway and give you a friend-zone handshake.

By the end of chapter one, your reader should know:

- what to expect from the book (magic, mystery, thriller etc.)

- what the main conflict is

- who most of the important players are

Don't forget to give your readers a hook; something to keep them attached to the character(s). Give them something to root for or against by the end of the chapter.

3-3. CHAPTER FOCUS

Each chapter is a mini book in and of itself. It serves a function, and when that function is complete, the chapter is complete. Therefore, it can be any size in length. You're going to want an opener (goal in mind), a rising action, and then a cliff-hanger ending for the chapter (to help drag the reader along to the next chapter).

No matter the information you want to convey, it *must* tie into the first opening paragraph (if it's the first chapter). Should it be any other chapter in the story, it *must* tie into the **plot**.

Let's say you have a character called Nancy, she's 40-ish, she works as a school nurse, she's never had a real boyfriend, and she's rather shy. She's now at a bank robbery.

None of that info is related. AT ALL. That's not bad, but you don't want to jump in there and give us her info bare, and then the scene. That's how data dumps are made. So how do you tie in the key info with the scene and keep the pace and tension?

You pepper it in.

A man in a ski mask barked, "Hit the ground!"

Nancy did just that. At forty-three, her knees weren't what they used to be, but as someone with a gun entered the bank, she cared less about how she'd get up, and more about not being dragged along as a human shield.

As the sirens closed in, she covered her head. Her heart pounded. One pop punctuated the air and then a body collapsed to the floor.

Blood dripped out right in front of her. As she stared into the dead eyes behind the mask, her life flashed.

Those forty-three years were all rather disappointing.

Fifteen years as a school nurse…rendered meaningless now.

What did she have to show for it? Never daring to do anything—be with anyone.

Pop. Pop. Pop.

Broken glass danced along the floor. She turned onto her side and crouched up into a ball. If she got out of this, she would give Stewart another chance. She'd take that trip to Fiji; she'd even bungee-jump. God, if she could make it out of this alive….

The information can go with the action, with the scene. Do not 'pause' and give it. Compare it to:

> Nancy was forty-three, a school nurse, and painfully shy and reserved.
>
> A man in a ski mask barked, "Hit the ground!"

When you give exposition to the reader, it will STOP all action. It's as if the characters all froze mid-motion, letting you tell the story around them. We don't want that unless it's a life-changing situation or an epiphany.

You could leave a cliffhanger for that scene by maybe having Nancy grab a gun, jump up, and shoot one of the bank robbers point blank. (end scene) What happens next? Ooww, that reader wants to know.

The second example for Nancy is common, it's also the reason 'was' raises red flags. If you're not sure if you've got a data dump or a clumsy sentence, should you say something like, "He was six-foot-three with blue eyes," then you could have done it smoother.

Let's say Nancy does shoot someone, escapes, and is now enjoying a drink on the beach while a manhunt is underway for her. She's being bolder, but we want to *show* these things without giving them as bare facts.

You can use this 'was' pattern to make a statement, however.

Try doing it in threes.

> He was six-foot-three, blue-eyed, and Nancy's next biggest mistake.

Otherwise, just putting it there to describe the character…is a bit flat.

Consider:

> He walked in, his toned six-foot-three figure towering over nearly everyone there. Tight jeans hugged strong thighs and Nancy nearly fainted when he turned to order a drink and she could see him from behind.

Now we know Nancy is an easily enticed pervert, and the guy is hot. Make your words count, and make every scene do double-duty—moving the plot, but fleshing out the characters.

3-4. Story Development

Even for veterans of the editing process, this aspect can be daunting. That is to say, cutting away entire scenes—sometimes entire chapters, is a tough thing to do.

At times, however, it's necessary. And with that in mind, an author going into the development edit without a strict editor will need to be even more unforgiving with regards to what stays or goes.

First thing to remember: it can't stay if it doesn't fit. Of course it would be lovely if your favorite areas stuck around, but it can't all stay. If you're lucky, the majority of it will remain, but chances are, you will need to jettison something. In some instances, you may have to add more. But your goal should be reduction. So let go of that safety blanket and instead…pick up that cutlass. It's time to *kill* the darlings.

Those cuts you did before? *Nothing* compared to the lacerations you're going to be responsible for now.

Reduction will tighten the pace.

Reduction will keep the plot moving.

Reduction will mean your plot hasn't run away with you.

Reduction, reduction, reduction. Adding is fine if something else gets taken out.

THE PLOT

You and your betas will hopefully decide if the plot is solid.

Here is a checklist of things that should be present in your story.

Your story needs:

- A clear conflict. What is it the character wants or needs? In the first chapter, something must happen to set this in motion.

- Clear knowledge of the consequences of failure. Tell the reader what's at stake. What is on the line if this character fails?

- A clear path to the character's goals. Even if the character fails, she should still be making that journey. Does the character have a plan?

- Introduce the other key players from chapter two but not after the halfway mark. Once you reach more than half-way through the book, new characters should not be popping up. If you have a character who will come later on, make mention of him often in the earlier chapters.

- Character development. Your main character must change and grow and learn from the experiences he's been through—to form either a positive or negative conclusion.

- A proper resolution of all conflicts by the end of the story. Of course, if the book will have a sequel some questions can remain open but make sure and close up a lot of other (major) questions presented in this book. Otherwise your reader will feel cheated: he/she has made this journey with your character, only to get no satisfaction once it's all said and done.

PLOT STRUCTURE

The good thing and bad thing about the structure of your plot is that it can come at any time. For most, it happens *after* the first draft. It's best if you tame it before sending it to an editor or beta reader. Otherwise you risk running off beta readers and losing money by having to go through the edit twice. So write your first draft without a plot if you have to, but your second draft *needs* a clear plot.

A story will consist of three Acts:

Beginning

Middle

and an End.

THE BEGINNING

Contrary to popular belief, the very beginning isn't the part for 'build-up.' It's a start. Imagine a gun going off and everyone starts to run the race. This is what your first chapter should be—the start.

Chapter 1: Something happens that sets this journey in motion. This can occur at the end of the chapter.

You have until the end of this one chapter to get your reader curious, or hooked, enough to continue. Sometimes you have even less than the first chapter. You have the first page; the first paragraph; the first line. Make your words count.

Let's use the film, Avatar©, as an example. In Avatar the hero wants to use his legs again so he comes on this journey. The inciting event is his entering the avatar of his twin brother. He's able to run again, and wants more.

Chapter 2: This might be your last chance to hook your reader if you haven't already. Most of the key players should start showing up from here. In this chapter, something happens to propel your character from his/her normal life.

The hero gets lost and is rescued by one of the natives of the planet.

Chapter 3: More secondary characters. By now the plot and consequences are clear and everything is set in motion.

They explore the world a little further. The main scientist has misgivings about the protagonist but puts up with him.

Chapter 4: Character is forced to make a choice (something that might change his/her life). The character might not know how important this decision is at the time.

One antagonist offers the hero the ability to walk once more if he helps gather intelligence on the natives. There is a place called Hometree which has the mineral the humans want.

Chapter 5: Consequences follow, good or bad. The journey begins.

The main character is transferred to a new outpost with other secondary characters when the scientist in charge learns of the deal they made.

Chapter 6-10: Complications as things get more involved.

The main character grows sympathetic to the natives, and a romance starts to form. The main character mates with one of the natives and attacks his fellow humans. His change of allegiance becomes clear and the other humans mobilize to intercept him.

THE MIDDLE

By now the journey's well on the way and although some things are going well, other things aren't. Getting to this point is the easy part, usually. But from here on out, this is where the story starts to take a new, fuller shape.

Chapter 11: A crisis forces the protagonist into a new direction. No new characters.

Humans are going to attack Hometree. The main character has to confess to being a spy. The natives must prepare for the attack.

Chapter 12 – 16: Things get more complex. There's no turning back for the character.

Humans attack, destroying Hometree. The leader of the tribe is killed. All scientists are detached from their avatars and imprisoned.

Chapter 17: New crisis or problem forces the protagonist into new complexities.

The humans decide to attack the Tree of Souls.

Chapter 18: Consequences of that new decision.

The main scientist is shot. The natives try to transfer her body into the avatar (foreshadowing), but she dies before they could succeed.

Chapter 19: The situation looks bad.

The main character subdues one of the strongest dragon-like creatures and tries to rally the other clans to fight in a seemingly unwinnable battle.

Chapter 20: Things go from bad to worse.

The natives suffer great casualties. The main character prays to the planet for help.

THE END

In the end, most if not all the issues brought up in the beginning and middle should find some resolution. The end of a book is just as important as the beginning. A reader must feel like the journey was worth it so tie up all loose ends.

Chapter 21: This seems like the protagonist's darkest moment(s).

Things look bleak until the planet's wildlife starts to fight back. The main character's current resting place (his human body) is threatened.

Chapter 22: Plot points tie in together to form a solid resolution where the character learns and grows.

With the planet's help, the humans are defeated. The main character is rescued. The bad guy is killed.

Chapter 23-24: Believable wrap up where points touched on in the first few chapters are addressed.

All humans leave except a select few. Then the main character's body is transferred into the avatar permanently and he has the abilities he'd longed for in chapter one.

This is a loose rundown. Fiddle around with it and see what works best. But this is a typical hero's journey. Avoid plot twists without proper foreshadowing. Once again, new characters should not be introduced after the midway point. By the end, the character must have grown or changed.

If you are unsure of the plot even after the first draft, don't worry. It happens. Just ask yourself, **"What is the problem? What is the possible solution? What is the actual solution?"**

As in Avatar, the basic problem is that the character can no longer walk. The possible solution is to take this job and spy on the native aliens of the planet. The actual solution is putting his consciousness into the body of his twin brother's avatar.

Much more is going on, of course, but this basic problem, possible solution, and actual solution remains true. Once you've singled out your most basic plot, write each chapter to come back to that problem, that possible solution, while foreshadowing the *actual* solution. *The attempt at trying to transfer the main scientist's consciousness to her avatar failed but it was foreshadowing.*

Keep in mind that this outline also applies to short stories and even children's stories. Take any children's movie and break it down. You will find these elements.

Beginning:

- conflict

- inciting incident

- life-changing decision (unaware of its significance)

- consequences of that decision (good or bad)

- things become complex

Middle:

- crisis

- new consequences

- more complexities (no turning back)

- new crisis

- change in direction

- consequences of that action

- things worsen (it all looks hopeless)

End:

- darkest moments

- all the plot points converge

- believable ending

Let's try this formula with a child's cartoon: Curious George© (the Movie).

Beginning:

- *conflict:* George is lonely. Ted's job is at risk.

- *inciting incident:* Ted goes to Africa to find an artifact.

- *life-changing decision:* Ted plays with a monkey. Ted sends a pic of the artifact instead of *saying* it's small. It looks huge in the picture. **He leaves his hat with the monkey.** George follows Ted home.

- *consequences of that decision:* Ted's boss has adverts all over NY for this artifact. It's a huge sensation. George turns his life upside down.

- *things become more complex:* Ted finds that the monkey he played with has followed him home. The monkey causes havoc.

Middle:

- *crisis*: Ted is kicked out of his house. He calls animal control for George: foreshadowing.

- *new consequences:* Discovers a way to make the artifact look big.

- *more complexities (no turning back)*: George destroys the machine to enlarge the artifact.

- *new crisis:* This is not present.

- change in direction: This is not present.

- consequences of that action: This is not present.

- *things worsen (it all looks hopeless)*: Ted loses his job. Animal control comes for George.

End:

- *darkest moments:* Ted misses George. He goes after him.

- *all the plot points converge:* On the way to Africa, Ted (with George's help) realizes the small artifact is in fact a map. They use it to find the real artifact which is huge.
- *believable ending:* The museum is saved and Ted gets his job back. George is no longer lonely.

Just because a story is short or of a different genre doesn't mean these key points aren't important. Of course, a lot more is going on in the stories listed above, but the bare essentials are these plot elements. In both examples I don't make much mention of the bad guys and other conflicts going on because they aren't the main plot points. Try to isolate your plot points that focus on the main characters rather than other characters.

BREAKING THE FOURTH WALL

Another thing to consider is *breaking the fourth wall.* It is understood that in a play or a story, there are three walls; the fourth wall is the audience. When the character or narrator addresses the reader directly, this is breaking the fourth wall. Some writers do it stylistically, but it's not always easy to do well.

There are pros and cons to it. Either way, be consistent.

Breaking the fourth wall can sometimes take the reader out of the story and ruin the fantasy. If the characters and even the narrator don't believe in the world, then it becomes difficult for the reader to take it seriously as well.

Still, some writers do this and do it expertly. If you are new to writing, it might be best to avoid this at first until you are comfortable enough to try it.

The best way to decide is by reading a book that uses this technique.

CHEKHOV'S GUN

Chekhov's gun is a dramatic principle that cannot be emphasized enough. It states that each and everything mentioned in the narrative *must* have a purpose. If a gun is hanging on the wall in chapter one, then eventually, in one of the subsequent chapters to follow, that gun *must* go off.

If your character passes by a dead homeless man with a needle in his arm more than once, then you must apply Chekhov's gun. If your character *talks* or otherwise interacts with another character that you give distinct features, you must apply Chekhov's gun. Everything you mention (especially if you go into great detail about it) must serve a purpose.

Make your words count. 90,000 words might seem like a lot, but it can quickly explode into disaster if Chekhov's gun isn't applied. A reader also assumes each thing mentioned will be of value later on. So don't focus on anything inconsequential. If it's not going to be used in the narrative later on (and it's got nothing to do with the price of tea in China…) don't give it too much detail. Move on.

On the first draft it's easy to put each and everything in. By the second draft, however, you should know what is necessary and what isn't. Anything that does not serve a greater purpose should be removed.

CHARACTERS

Enough can't be said about staying away from Mary Sue characters. Most characters will have something about them that is similar to the author. It's common for the creator of something to infuse said creation with a part of themselves. When that character seems like a daydreamed, carbon copy, or is incredibly *perfect*, incredibly *imperfect*, a great victim or tragedy, or downright infallible, the character is a **Mary Sue**.

It's good to write what you know. It's good to give the characters flaws. It's good to give the characters good features. There is one thing the character(s) need: **balance**.

OTHER THINGS TO REMEMBER

- Don't leave your characters idle.

- Don't let them whine.

- Give them redeeming qualities.

- Give them flaws.

- Give them vices to overcome.

- Give them actual conflicts.

- Give them dialogue that matches their *age*, timeline, and setting. A forty-year-old man in New York City in 2015 will not say, "Golly, son, that's a heavy satchel you've got there," unless he's a time traveler. A people who have no reference to God cannot use words referring to God, etc., etc. Make it all match.

3-5. SHOWING VS. TELLING

Showing versus Telling is a big problem for a lot of people. On a first draft, telling can save an author a lot of time. Telling can keep the writing pace of that draft moving. And of course, telling is sometimes a habit.

Please remember: telling is fine…to a point.

We've already established that your first chapter is like a first date. Your POV is the area where the reader looks out at this new world. The rest is the meat.

Now and then, an author might finish what he believes to be an *epic* story, only to discover it was *barely* half the size he had expected.

Chances are the reason for that is too much telling.

If a child came up to you and asked,

"What is a rainbow?"

105

You could look her in the eye and let her know,

> "According to the dictionary: a rainbow is an arc or circle that exhibits in concentric bands the colors of the spectrum and that is formed opposite the sun by the refraction and reflection of the sun's rays in raindrops, spray, or mist."

Now, it wouldn't be wrong, but it would be boring.

The alternative is to turn on the sprinklers, and show a small rainbow when the sun meets that water.

Showing also helps readers interact with your story. It does a lot of heavy lifting that telling cannot do. More importantly, it keeps things *active*.

Consider:

> The arki food was a bitter fruit that left the eater howling for days, crying out for a suris blossom.

This telling is good. It gives the reader much-needed information. In fact, maybe the reader now wants to know what a **suris blossom** is.

So give the reader more:

The arki food was a bitter fruit that left the eater howling for days, crying out for a suris blossom. As suris blossoms only grew in cold areas, they would have to climb Mt. Luff to reach it. At this time of night it would take them too long to get there and back. When Lance was a child, he'd found one by mistake and longed to see another ever since. He was eager to start his search.

Did you retain all of that? The new names? The new landscape? This is information the audience needs, but it's bare fact that is likely to be skimmed, if that.

Interact with your reader. Show us this information. Grow your scene.

Here is an example of how to show. It is a far longer scene but showing has a tendency to flesh stories out.

Suggestion:

"I wouldn't if I were you…" Lance warned.

Belle cut him a glance. A smug smile in place, she took a bite to spite him.

A sweet yet tangy taste filled her mouth. She let out a gasp as she regarded the purple pulp. "This is incredible."

107

Sitting back on a rock, Lance crossed his arms. "I honestly wouldn't if I were you—"

Too late, she ate more—and more and more still.

Each mouthful was better than the last until she took one bite and…nothing. There was no sensation, no taste.

When she swallowed that time, her throat burned like eating sand.

"What…what's happening?"

"Told you," Lance sang. "Wait for it…the best is yet to come."

A warm sensation came into her neck, and then one heave sent the purple seeds spilling on the ground.

"Mother of the Gods!" Belle retched again. "It burns!"

"The arki fruit is better when ripe. Overripe, well…." Lance shrugged. "This is *overripe*."

"How do I stop it? Please stop it," Belle begged.

When Lance didn't answer, she feared he'd left.

"Please stop it!"

"Well, it must hurt for a princess like you to beg that much."

Cold metal pressed against her lips.

"Drink," Lance said. "Water will help for now."

Palming the flask, she swallowed as much as she could before it became unbearable.

"Easy. Easy now."

Belle pleaded, "The suris blossoms. Give me the suris blossom!"

"Sad news, I'm afraid. The blossom we currently have is that of a suris lookalike. The real ones only grow in the cold. We cannot afford to climb that far up the mountain in the dead of night—if we can find one at all. There were more when I was young. Your people cursed them. Fortunately, you can undo that curse."

The burning of Belle's face faded, but not entirely. She opened her eyes.

Lance gestured to Mt. Luff. "That's the only place I know. We'll wait till sunrise, but then we must hurry. An overripe arki fruit will kill a man in two days."

Belle's eyes widened. "What?"

"Oh, a fit one does grant one power temporarily. Just not this one." Lance shrugged.

"Then *why* did you allow me to eat it?"

"Allow you? Like anyone can stop you. And I'd think the reason would be pretty obvious by now, lady—I wasn't necessarily sent to come to your rescue. You have something I want, and I suggest you follow my orders from now on. Are we clear? Because by now I think it's rather easy to see; I *know* how to hurt one of you."

A few things happened when the scene is fleshed out. One paragraph turned into pages. This is how it no doubt played out in your head as you drafted, but that's not how it translated when you started to *tell*.

Showing vs. telling does a lot of things for the author. It allows you to show the personality of the characters. Their reactions paint their personality. By now we can all agree Belle is stubborn, arrogant, rash, maybe young, and certainly pampered.

We also get to see Lance in a lot of different ways. These aren't real characters for any sort of book; they were created solely for this demonstration.

By fleshing out a scene, the author can also determine *why* this information is necessary. *Why* the reader must know all these things.

Every word has to count so it is best to avoid information that won't be useful later on; and *certainly* don't name something unless you plan to use it again somewhere else. As you draft, you won't be sure what you'll need, but eventually as you edit, you can know by then if you never follow up on XYZ, therefore, it can be sacrificed.

This scene can also read differently from Lance's POV. It might be shorter. And you're allowed to pepper in a few telling things here and there. Let's keep it in Belle's POV and throw some telling in there—the good sort.

e.g.,

> Belle stared at him. She wanted to wrap her hands around his thick neck and squeeze. "Then *why* did you allow me to eat it?"

And keep in mind that if we are in Belle's POV, we can get some of her inferences.

Consider:

> "Allow you?" Lance laughed like the idiot he was. "Like anyone can stop you. And I'd think the reason would be pretty obvious by now, lady—I wasn't necessarily sent to come to your rescue. You have something I want, and I suggest you follow my orders from now on. Are we clear? Because by now I think it's rather easy to see; I *know* how to hurt one of you."

Of course, Lance isn't calling himself an idiot. This is Belle's perception of him. In fact, if she compared him to a tree, should the scene be in her POV, she can use those terms to refer to him again and again. This is a nice way to pepper in details without going the telling route.

Consider:

> "Allow you?" Lance laughed like the idiot he was. "Like anyone can stop you." He lumbered toward her, his thick thighs rubbing together.
>
> She took him in for a moment. Despite their two days of travel, this was the first time she noticed part of his right ear was missing. Her skin warmed at the thought that she had ever considered him handsome.
>
> He came face to face with her. A sour smell seeped through those rotten teeth. "And I'd think the reason would be pretty obvious by now, lady—I wasn't necessarily sent to come to your rescue. You have something I want, and I suggest you follow my orders from now on. Are we clear? Because by now I think it's rather easy to see; I *know* how to hurt one of you."

The picture of Lance is getting clearer, and clearer still all without the pace slowing too much. We needed a pause for effect, and got that pause by sharing some details about him.

Remember, everyone has a style, so fiddle around with it until you find your own. Break the rules now and then, but not too often if you can help it. And show rather than tell.

Other shorter examples:

Telling: "How do you feel?" she asked seductively. (Adverbs tell rather than show)

vs.

Showing: She leaned in and brushed her lips along his ear. "How do you feel?"

She could also put her hand on his face, his knee, etc. to show intimacy. In reality, we use a lot of motion, cues, and expressions to convey our feelings and intent. Try to employ those in your scene. *Show* your characters' emotion.

Another example:

Telling: Ms. Lobal was a cruel woman.

vs.

Showing: Ms. Lobal smiled when she heard I was injured.

Flesh out your scene. No need to add more chapters to that epic draft. Turns out, you might have a huge scene where you least expect it.

So slow it down…and flesh it out.

Caution:

> This will take practice and everyone's guilty of it to some degree, but avoid *As You Know, Captain*. When one character tells another character something he/she *already* knows, this is referred to as *As You Know, Captain*. This is an info dump disguised as showing. Authors sometimes feel clever when they put this in but instead, it's rather transparent and *telling*. Characters talking to one another is a great way to convey information, but don't repeat something they both know (for the benefit of the reader)—at least, don't be obvious about it.

PEPPERING IN DETAILS

For a lot of us, a phrase that starts "Ms. Lobal was a short, heavyset woman with wide eyes and a pleasing smile," seems fine. Stylistically, it can work. The problem is that it's rare an author will stop just there.

Authors often feel compelled to tack on detail after detail which slows down the story and causes a lagging effect.

Peppering in detail can be done without sacrificing the pace.

Consider:

Jamie watched Ms. Lobal waddle around her desk, her wide thighs grazing the mahogany as she lowered herself into her chair with an audible, "Ahh."

"Good grief, my feet hurt," Ms. Lobal announced. "So dear…." One black pump clanged on the floor as the woman took to rubbing her meaty right foot. "How can I help you? I told Mr. Porter I'd have no time to feed the homeless this month, so I hope you haven't come looking for a free meal."

Eyes fixed on those crooked toenails—one was black and looked as if it threatened to fall right off—Jamie struggled to listen.

"What? Oh, oh yes." Jamie sat up, smoothing out her lumpy frock. She'd gotten the wrong size after all; the shoulder areas kept falling off.

The way Ms. Lobal eyed that dress told Jamie all she needed to know; the woman was set on saying, "No."

"Um, never mind, ma'am," Jamie said, lumbering to her feet. The dress fluffed even more. She looked ridiculous.

Ms. Lobal's stifled chuckle must have meant she thought the same.

115

Head held high—as high as she dared hold it lest she stumble in these tight shoes—Jamie marched out of that office.

There wasn't much left of her dignity, and when she closed that door only to hear Ms. Lobal's muffled cackle, the last of it faded.

This example uses as few instances of 'was' as possible. Once again, 'was' is no monster. Often times it is harmless, but now and again it can be indicative of a mini-data dump or something that can be peppered in a bit more smoothly.

Even that last part can change:

Her dignity waned, but when she closed that door only to hear Ms. Lobal's muffled cackle, the last of it faded.

3-6. GETTING FEEDBACK

Overall, it turns out, human beings aren't awful creatures. From a young age we are taught to be polite. The old adage of, "If you can't say something nice, don't say anything at all," is something you are bound to encounter. Meaning that sometimes you send out your manuscript, asking for feedback, and you *never* hear back from anyone.

Firstly, remember, nobody is out to get you. The bad things they say aren't because they hate you and somehow want to take great pleasure in your pain.

True, there are some who can't say *anything* positive. Others still are so bitter about their own failings that they can't help but put someone down, no matter how hard they try. Even with all that in mind, the vast majority of people *truly* want you to succeed. When they agree to look at your work, they often mean no harm.

In an effort not to hurt you or disappoint you, they disappear into the night. Those are better than the polar opposites: the lazy readers who *never* have anything *bad* to say. They are dangerous and should be avoided at all costs.

The goal of a *content edit* is to find plot holes, fix flat or useless characters, tighten up that flow, and more importantly, make sure the piece is readable.

You can do a cost-effective content edit purely on feedback. This is good if you have a solid draft. This isn't as great if you have a shaky draft and need professional help to hammer it out.

Don't give up, though, there are others willing to help you if you keep looking. Assuming you have a completed draft, let's continue to the next step: **looking for beta readers.**

THINGS TO REMEMBER

#1 Don't ever send your full manuscript to a random stranger. Although the idea of theft is a bit farfetched (even well-established authors have been plagiarized and chances are, your piece is too rough to be worthwhile, anyway), it is still something to consider.

The second reason for not sending out your entire manuscript is because you don't know if this beta reader is going to help you all that much. In the off chance that the manuscript isn't terrible, the reader might read it through and hardly provide you with any real feedback.

To start, send one to three chapters. You can determine whether or not to continue from there. This is also helpful to the beta reader because he/she doesn't feel pressured to do the impossible (try to read an entire manuscript that's difficult to get through).

How you choose to provide your entire manuscript from then on is up to you. Some people use PDF, some use regular doc file. Keep in mind that any loose format you send can be converted to something else. The doc format is good because a beta reader might put inline comments which are very useful.

#2 Don't take a negative review to heart. This does *not* mean you should ignore it. Never ignore a review, no matter who it's from—even a troll. Go back through the feedback and do so with an open mind. Imagine it's coming from a friend who means you no harm, not a random stranger. If they made valid arguments, adjust your manuscript accordingly. If they made harsh comments but don't explain them, should you feel the claims are unhelpful, then you can disregard them. Anyone who cannot back up their claim with an explanation is not showing much credibility.

#3 It's okay to be upset. It's normal to even cry or want to throw something when you get feedback and it's less than stellar. Take a break for a bit and read it again. Even if it was what you considered mean, know that feedback is like sandpaper, sometimes it's abrasive and it hurts but using it to your advantage is the best you can do with it. Don't give up.

#4 Don't deal with jerks. Just because you're asking for feedback doesn't mean you are advocating being harassed or abused. Beta reader feedback shouldn't have to come with a safe word. If you honestly feel uncomfortable with this reader, try another. But if you see a trend of reader after reader mentioning the same shortcomings, please consider there may be a real problem you need to address.

#5 Never use just one source. When you shop around for the best item, best deal, best house, you never go to one source. This is also the case in editing. You want beta reader*s*, a decent amount.

#6 *Read* the fiction of your readers. Should your reader write as well then take the advice as it comes. Most people cannot tell you *why* a manuscript is bad, just that it is. If your reader is also an author, however, *read* something from that author. Often times, an author with poor writing habits might not be able to judge your piece well as they can't judge their own. You can gauge just how objective and factual the critique is based on reading that author's work as well.

#7 Read the works of others—WIP (works in progress) or published. You may not want to. You may conjure up all sorts of excuses, a popular one being, "I don't want it to contaminate my writing." It won't contaminate your writing. If you truly want to be original, then read as many books as you can. This is the best way to avoid using a similar plot, while keeping your individuality. Otherwise you might write a lot of books without having read others, only to end up with nearly the same plot. That's because we live in the same times and often have subconscious influences that will come through in our writing. So please read.

#8 Don't buy into feedback that is all-flattering. Giving praise is very easy and it means less work for a reader. Make a checklist of questions you want to ask the beta reader, and give it over along with the first chapter. Yes, you want people to like it. Yes, the goal is to get it praised. However, during the editing phase, that won't do you a great deal of good. It will build up your ego, but not much else. If it's all rosy and perfect, ask some questions. If you get no direct answers, be suspicious. Get a second opinion or a third. That warm hand patting you on the rump might be that of a lazy and/or spiteful troll. Say it with me, "All good feedback without a hint of criticism = bad touch."

#9 If you haven't cried at least *once*, then you probably haven't gotten any honest critiques.

Once you have your feedback, apply the changes and find new betas until finally, you have a few people who can read through the entire thing without pause. Rinse and repeat.

Keep in mind:

Once you go through a few rounds of edits and feedback, it's all right to ask the latest beta readers for a review once they make it all the way to the end. Be prepared, though. Just because they liked it does not mean a five-star review—and that's a *good* thing. You want honesty. Start picking up reviews as early as you can. Be sure to ask beta readers to identify themselves as such in the review.

THE BENEFIT OF BETA READERS

Allowing others to sample your work is a good way to attract others to it. For some reason, a lot of people like to see a book in the making.

Sometimes, if they like your work, they might check out your other books on their own.

Should you go through the process, then I suggest sending a few chapters. Get your feedback, and decide whether or not to send more. Chances are the first few chapters will be so rough you'll have to make deep edits before sending it out again. That is far better than just sending your work into the unknown, never knowing what came of it.

- Be respectful to your beta readers.

- Don't argue with them about your content.

- Don't defend your work. Your defense of your work was your entire work. That was your chance. Not after the fact.

- Don't brush off their feedback. *Think* about it first.

- Ask questions to make sure this feedback is solid (good or bad feedback as it may be).

- Don't take gushing feedback at face value (bad touch). Ask questions, get second or third opinions.

- Make a check-list and send it with your manuscript.

CHECKLIST OF QUESTIONS TO ASK

Beta readers (not to be confused with ALPHA readers: readers of a rough-draft) test drive your work. They are 'beta testing' your book. The manuscript you show them should be in good shape, minimal typos etc. etc. Their focus is content and the plot.

Although a good beta reader will give you a lot of feedback, more still aren't sure *how* to give feedback. Some don't think they are qualified to. By making a list of questions and sending it along with your manuscript, you make their task much easier.

Have them take a look before they start. Remind them to *stop whenever they want*, and keep your fingers crossed. Remember; send only your first chapter (or first three) to start. *Do not send your entire manuscript into the unknown.*

List of questions:

- Is this your usual genre?

- Did the first line catch your attention?

- Was the first paragraph strong?

- Did you care about the character(s)?

- Did the first chapter have a hook (Something to make you burn to read chapter two)?

- Did it lag anywhere (feel sluggish or otherwise dry)?

- Were the characters believable?

- Was there anything you expected that didn't happen?

- Where do you think the story is going?

- How was the dialogue overall?

- How was the pace overall?

- Did you stop part way? And why?

- Would you read chapter two? Why? Why not?

- Anything you hated?

- Anything you really liked?

BOOK BLURBS

Here is a challenging area that's sure to induce more than a few shudders. Book blurbs can bring a grown person to tears by either being *very* easy or...*very, very* hard.

Again, most human beings are actually quite polite. They will almost always try to find the good things about your blurbs. Casual readers won't be as forgiving.

People do judge a book by its cover. So when you are posting a cover and looking for blurb feedback, consider using some distance.

How?

Go into a writing forum and post a topic requesting feedback. Here's a suggestion: rather than say it's your own blurb, say it is the blurb of 'a friend.' Also, do not shed a negative or positive light on it. You don't want to elicit people poking fun for the heck of it. And you don't want to elicit compliments. Instead, you want honesty (or a semblance of it because art is really subjective.)

Here is the recommended phrase:

> "This is my best friend's new book cover. She wants my thoughts on it, but I want to get some second and third opinions."

The end. Nothing else. No 'hints' as to your own thoughts, views, or what you are leaning toward.

P.S. it would be beneficial if you do not post it with your own name on the cover.

Be mindful of your reaction. Remember, people are just being honest (for themselves). Ultimately, you should decide on the blurb and cover you want, but the function of a blurb is to attract readers. This also works for objective book cover feedback in general.

4. PROOFREADING

Proofreading is an area where a lot of authors do pay a little something. It's almost a mini line edit. It won't fix a lot of things the line edit is for, but it will take care of superficial spots.

There's a problem with proofreading, though. From the expensive to cheap (and I've had both), no one proofreader is going to be able to catch each and every typo.

Even one book that went through two proofreaders still had one or two stragglers.

So how can you proofread your book for a good price, or cheap?

A good proofreader isn't just a reader. He or she is an editor. They are able to spot misplaced punctuation, misused words, etc. etc. because they edit and that's what they are paid for.

If you do go with an editor, it's more advisable that you get a different one for each stage of the edit. Likewise, you'll need a new one for the proofread as the other edits have stolen the editor's objectivity.

Let's assume you used beta readers for content. That is all right. Beta readers can also find typos, though that isn't necessarily fair because there isn't money in it for the beta reader.

A beta-read proofread isn't a bad thing because you can get multiple eyes looking your draft over.

Assuming you are going the cheapest route possible, consider stepping away from the story for a month or two so that you, too, can read the print copy with fresh eyes.

It might be best if you get a physical proof to read, also. Typos are easier to catch in new formats.

Get 'text to speech' enabled in MS Word, Open Office, Libre Office, etc. This is a robotic voice and it is not perfect, but it will read your text to you.

Whether or not you go the free or cost-effective route, please also consider a **Typo Party Contest**.

WHAT'S A TYPO PARTY?

A Typo Party is more of a competition than a party. I've employed it in the past with success. Even this book will have been proofread a final time via a Typo Party Contest.

The slogan is:

Read

Nab

Win

Before you hold a contest, it is *imperative* that your betas, or others, proofread this book for you. This does *not* replace proofreading. Rather, it complements it.

In this contest, readers are given the ARC (Advanced Reviewer Copy) of the final, proofed draft.

Participants read it casually (not for the sake of a proofread or an edit). A casual read reminds them they have every opportunity to stop whenever they choose.

They document any typos they find then submit it to you. Whoever has the most typos at the end of the contest wins.

The prize can be a small monetary amount (from $30-$50). Other prizes can involve paperback copies, or the winner's name in a book as a character. Why no extravagant prize? Because then it becomes a job. The main idea behind this is that readers *read* for fun. In return, they get a free ARC they might enjoy. And they can stop at any time.

For second and third place, you can offer another prize, like the final eBook or a small gift card.

There are several advantages to a Typo Party Contest.

> - Exposure. People have never heard of it and get curious to see what it's about when they might have otherwise overlooked you.

> - Competition. Some people honestly just like to win at something. Others still are just very resentful of typos in general and want to help.

> - Reviews. You can ask for a review. A lot of people honestly will give it.

> - A final, *final* proofread by *many*, many people. Sometimes these contests show simple typos that escaped. Your book can be as **typo-free** as possible.

Advertise well in advance (e.g., one month or more).

A Typo Party Contest was conducted for *In Liam's Wake: The Makeshift Soldier I.*

Depending on how you distribute the final version for the Typo Party, you might get a pretty good turnout.

There are some methods online that involve a no 'copy and paste' feature which is a good way to have peace of mind if you are truly worried.

Another way to distribute is to send a doc file *directly* to someone's kindle email address. Mention it in the contest rules that they should add your email address (the one you will send the file from) to the 'safe' list on the kindle website.

You can pick up some reviews and maybe feedback before going live with your book.

An Alternative:

> Another method is to go live with a thoroughly proofread book on kindle and (if you are eligible for a free promotion via KDP select) offer the eBook free in correlation with a Typo Party Contest. Include a disclaimer in the first few pages. After a couple of days, set the eBook at $0.99 rather than free.

Once the contest is complete, upload the new version and contact Amazon to request that they update all previous copies (if you'd like). New copies will have the updated version. In this case, you can put it at normal price rather than $0.99.

HOW TO DO IT

The key of the Typo Party is to get people talking. They can say good things or bad things, but get people talking.

On your author homepage, make a post (or page) called 'contest.'

Create a form (you can do so on google docs), asking participants several questions. Here are some of the fields.

Name

Email Address

Is this your first Typo Party?

What do you think of the idea?

Would you be willing to write a review?

What convinced you to participate?

Are you familiar with the author?

Save these email addresses for later. You will want to notify them when the time comes.

Detail just how much the first place winner gets, second place winner, etc. (Suggestion: First place is the money, and name in a book—if the book is fiction—the second place winner gets a free copy of the edited version if they review. Third place is up to you; maybe a thank you page mention.)

Contact a few of your Facebook writing groups, especially the ones where you are most active, and ask if they would pin your topic. Some groups are very generous and do so. Even for a few days would be momentous.

This book was given a Typo Party Contest advertised in *Writers' Group* on Facebook. The Typo Party for *In Liam's Wake: The Makeshift Soldier I* was pinned in the largest *unofficial NaNoWriMo* group on Facebook, despite me competing— and failing—in the NaNo only once, in 2013. No, *In Liam's Wake: The Makeshift Soldier I* wasn't a NaNo novel. At the time, I had no idea what NaNo was, just that people wrote a lot. They still allowed me to advertise for Liam's Typo Party Contest.

Most writing forums *want* to help you. You just need to ask. The unofficial NaNoWriMo group on facebook and Writers' Group were very generous and supportive to do so.

If they cannot pin your post about the Typo Party Contest, ask them to create an event for you instead. If an admin creates the event, all members are given a notice of it. If you create it yourself, only your friends within the group can receive the notice.

Start advertising for it about a month in advance. Spread the word, have friends help you. For this, you will need Facebook banners that are eye-catching.

Continue your edits. Make sure you get the book proofread, either by a professional or a number of people. There are several sites that are used for magazines (these sites don't allow copy and paste) so if you need a great deal of people to see it for a proofread but not copy it, I recommend that you find those.

When the time for the Typo Party Contest comes around, split the doc into two. Post one everyone can see (on the magazine, no copy & paste enabling site).

Give a deadline to get those typos in. You can set a private link to the latter half for anyone who turns in their typos. Make sure and give out this detail beforehand.

After all the typos are submitted, tally them up and make the corrections. Announce the winner. I sometimes give my second place winner a gift if I can or treat the other contestants.

So far, the best results were for the contest held for thirty full days. However you do it, it's still a number of eyes on your work. Be consistent and keep your deadlines. Give yourself about two weeks to review the typos and announce the winner(s).

     1. Write

     2. Edit

     3. Proofread

     4. Contest

5. EDIT FOR FREE?

The only way to truly edit for free would be to use these methods *slowly*. Take your time to do it all correctly.

But is it really all right to edit this way and without putting any money down anywhere?

That's a tough question. The only advantage is that readers aren't always writers, but writers are often readers. Another writer will spot your mistakes or shortcomings much sooner. They might not be able to carry on because you've missed a comma.

For the most part, a reader is only interested in a smooth read and a good story. If you can provide both of those, you should be all right.

So I guess the answer is…if you can take it for what it is, then yes, you can edit for free. If your goal is to make it readable and smooth, then yes. If you clear out as many typos as you can and weave a story that keeps the reader focused on the events, then yes.

Take it slow. Take months. Take your time and do it right. Don't try to do the impossible and do it right away. Respect the craft and respect your readers. If you don't put out much effort, please don't ask people to pay actual money to read something unpolished.

Another bit of advice is this: if you have a book you've written before that isn't well-edited, either unpublish it or edit it. When a potential reader tries to find you, he will judge you based on your previous work as well. A rough book 'just lying around' can do serious damage to your reputation.

Whatever method you choose, be it self-editing only, professional editing only, or a combination of the two, *please edit*.

Too often books with great potential get served to the audience still half-baked. It's a wasted chance.

6. CHOOSING AN EDITOR

From the topic and purpose of this book, one might think it's meant to challenge professional editing or otherwise. That is not the case. The bottom line is…editing is expensive.

But then again, editing *should* be expensive.

I worked part-time (mother of two kids with a full-time job) to pay for editing and book covers when I first started out. I had a lot of expectations and I was sure, with the proper steps, the investment would pay off.

The thousands gone from that endeavor aren't ones I regret even once. There's more going on here, however. Fake editors are very, *very* abundant. By the time an author figures it out, it's still time and money lost.

Here is the truly strange thing about it: it's not insidious. It's not intended as a con or a scam. These fake editors genuinely try their best. It's just that their best hasn't equated to the realization that being well-read does not an editor make.

And although I know others dispute the amount and even ask for refunds, I don't believe that's fair. If a bricklayer does a poor job, you might not realize it for a while, and you still pay.

When you hire an editor, you pay for their skill. If their skill is somewhat subpar, they still did the work the best they could and deserve a fair wage. I think a bit of feedback to them is in order, as well, but most won't stop trying to edit.

Due to the cost of publishing, this book hopes to spare others those problems.

But if you go with a professional editor, *please* vet that editor first.

THINGS TO REMEMBER

- Good editors almost *always* have work. This isn't always true but it's true enough. If you encounter an editor hungry for money, tread lightly.
- Cheap edits equal *bad* edits.
- Expensive edits don't promise good edits.
- A good editor doesn't mean a bestseller.

- Take on one editor for each stage of the process. Don't put all your eggs in one basket.
- Brush up on your grammar. Doing so will help you spot fake editors faster.
- READ. Even if it's the WIP (work in progress) of others. Read. Read and find out what works and what doesn't. Read and give feedback and learn to take feedback as well.
- Always ask for a book he/she has edited so you can read it for yourself. If the editor is a writer, ask for one of their books.
- Stay away from editors with a heavy workload who still take you on. Chances are, they cut costs and the edits are sloppy, anyway.
- Get a sample edit.
- An editor who doesn't treat you well even in email correspondences, won't bother treating you well once he/she has your money.
- Be cautious of finding editors in open forums.
- *Ask* questions.
- Leave errors in a sample piece and see how many the editor finds.
- Don't bother with an editor who brags about being harsh (you want a professional, not a jerk).
- Don't bother with an editor who promises you no tears (This editor is too soft and a waste of your time or a straight out liar.)

- Most freelance editors cannot meet deadlines well. Be cautious of those who never meet a single deadline. They might be unreliable.

However you finally select an editor, remember *one* very important thing: a good editor isn't just about changing your words. It isn't even rewriting your work for you. **A good editor will *use* your words, rearrange them and make them work. If you get a sample edit back and it's lost all your style, that editor has failed.** It should be an improved piece, however, still sound like it was written by you.

All throughout the professional editing process, you should still expect to do a lot of those edits yourself, following your editor's instructions and guidance.

7. FORMATTING

Formatting is so time-consuming and unpleasant that if someone does charge, I think it is worth paying for. But in an effort to keep with the cost-effective approach, let's dive in together.

On whatever program you use, no doubt you use the good ole-fashioned '**B**' for bold, '*I*' for italics, and '<u>U</u>' for underline. These are not recommended.

Sure, for emphasizing your words here and there, please use these direct features. *However*, when formatting your entire manuscript with things like chapter titles etc. please do not use these main buttons.

And whatever you do, do *not* use the dreaded… 'TAB' button.

The tab button can cause serious formatting issues for your manuscript when you try to publish it.

Something called 'Styles' is your new best friend. Find the 'Styles' menu, and start assigning features to the styles.

You have a specific style for the book name; one for the author; one for the copyright; one for the chapters, and so on. The good thing is that you can save these styles and use them for *every* book you ever write. So once they are set, you can essentially forget about them.

Also, be sure to choose a style for 'normal text.'

Here's the advantage. Let's say you have headings that are big, but regular text that are not. You want to change *all* normal text to either a new font or a new size. You only have to go into the *style* and fiddle with it there. Now *all* normal text changes. Same goes for titles, secondary titles, etc.

Get the page margins and dimensions from your paperback publisher (or Print On Demand publisher). Do all the changes there. When you are ready to upload this file, you can use that *same* file for both the paperback *and* the eBook.

Be mindful if you hire someone to help you format, though, because not everyone uses 'styles' and you might not be able to recreate whatever they've done on your own.
Meaning…you must pay each and every time and that can be costly.

Anyone can format alone. It just takes patience and practice.

8. WARNING: FOR NANOWRIMO

The NaNoWriMo (National Novel Writing Month: November) is a great way for an author to let the juices flow and write at a constant rate—all this while being cheered on by thousands of others in the same boat.

As you can imagine, it's a pretty intense time. It comes at a price, however, the goal of this event is not truly to write a novel, but rather…write a draft.

No novel is ever created in thirty days' time.

The true danger also comes with the main goal, "Write 50,000 words in one month."

With this, the focus isn't on the story, or hammering out all the kinks. It's about numbers. A set numbered goal that everyone is trying to meet.

Because the emphasis is put on quantity over quality (which is fine for a rough draft), the finished product requires a lot more objective scrutiny.

That is why I suggest waiting longer with NaNo novels before editing: maybe a year or more.

In the end, the final decision will fall to the author, of course, but this is only a friendly reminder.

Also, rather than wait for November, it's a good idea to try to write something daily whenever possible.

Regardless, writing, or attempting to write so much in such a short amount of time is truly an amazing feat. Congratulations to all the winners. Good luck.

THANK YOU

Thank you for reading this book. If you could take the time out to review it, I'd greatly appreciate it.

Good luck on your journey toward publication, whether traditionally or independently.

ABOUT THE AUTHOR

Ashlyn Forge is an independent author who has self-published several novels, short stories, and novellas. She also writes under the pseudonym Lyna Forge. Her preferred genre is science fiction & fantasy with romance.

Find out more at AshlynForge.com

OTHER WORKS BY THIS AUTHOR

If you liked this book, you may also like "The Ruins We Cherish," by the same author.

Other works include novels written under the pseudonym Lyna Forge such as "We Can Go Back."

INDEX